Bath Sets™

General Information

Many of the products used in this pattern book can be purchased from local craft, fabric and variety stores, or from the Annie's Attic Needlecraft Catalog (see Customer Service information on page 28).

Blue Waters
Bath Set
DESIGNS BY JANE PEARSON

TANK LID COVER
SKILL LEVEL

◖◼◼◻
INTERMEDIATE

FINISHED SIZE
Fits standard-size commode tank lid

MATERIALS
- Medium (worsted) weight yarn:
  5 oz/250 yds/142g variegated blue
  2 oz/100 yds/57g light periwinkle
- Size G/6/4mm crochet hook
  or size needed to obtain gauge
- Sewing needle
- Sewing thread
- Narrow elastic: 1 yd

4 MEDIUM

GAUGE
4 dc = 1 inch; 2 dc rows = 1 inch

PATTERN NOTES
Chain-3 at beginning of row or round counts as first double crochet unless otherwise stated.

Join with slip stitch as indicated unless otherwise stated.

SPECIAL STITCH
Knot stitch (knot st): Tr in next st, sc in next st.

INSTRUCTIONS
COVER
Row 1: With variegated blue, ch 95, dc in 4th ch from hook (*first 3 chs count as first dc*), dc in each rem ch across, turn. (*93 dc*)

Rows 2–9: Ch 3 *(see Pattern Notes)*, dc in each st across, turn. At end of last row, fasten off.

Row 10 (WS): Join light periwinkle with sc in first st, **knot st** *(see Special Stitch)* across, **do not turn**. Fasten off.

Tr should bend toward the RS of the work.

Row 11: Join light periwinkle with sc in first st at beg of last row, knot st across, turn. Fasten off.

Row 12: With RS facing, **join** *(see Pattern Notes)* variegated blue in first st, ch 3, dc in each rem st across, turn.

Rows 13–20: Ch 3, dc in each st across, turn. At end of last row, **do not turn**.

Rnd 21: Now working in rnds, ch 1, evenly sp 36 sc across ends of rows, working in starting ch on opposite side of row 1, sc in each st across, evenly sp 36 sc across ends of rows, sc in each st across row 20, join in beg sc.

Rnd 22: Ch 4, sk next st, [dc in next st, ch 1, sk next st] around, join in 3rd ch of beg ch-4. Fasten off.

FINISHING

Cut elastic to fit under rim of commode tank lid.

Weave elastic through sts on last rnd.

Sew or tie ends tog.

TISSUE BOX COVER
SKILL LEVEL
■■■□ **INTERMEDIATE**

FINISHED SIZE
Fits 4¾ x 9½ x 3-inch box of tissues

MATERIALS
- Medium (worsted) weight yarn:
  4 oz/200 yds/113g variegated blue
  2 oz/100 yds/57g light periwinkle
- Size G/6/4mm crochet hook or size needed to obtain gauge
- Tapestry needle

4 MEDIUM

GAUGE
4 sc = 1 inch; 4 sc rows = 1 inch

PATTERN NOTE
Join with slip stitch as indicated unless otherwise stated.

SPECIAL STITCH
Knot stitch (knot st): Tr in next st, sc in next st.

INSTRUCTIONS
COVER
TOP
MAKE 2.

Row 1: With variegated blue, ch 40, sc in 2nd ch from hook, sc in each ch across, turn. Fasten off. *(39 sc)*

Row 2 (WS): Join light periwinkle with sc in first st, **knot st** *(see Special Stitch)* across, turn. Fasten off.

Tr should bend toward the RS of the work.

Row 3: Join variegated blue with sc in first st, sc in each st across, turn. Fasten off.

Row 4: Join light periwinkle with sc in first st, knot st across, turn. Fasten off.

Row 5: Join variegated blue with sc in first st, sc in each st, across, turn.

Rows 6–10: Ch 1, sc in each st across, turn. At end of last row, fasten off.

Match bottom of row 1 on each piece tog, sew 6 sts at each end of matched edges tog leaving middle sts unsewn for center opening.

SIDES

Rnd 1: Now working in rnds around outer edge of assembled Cover Top, join variegated blue with sc in last st of row 10 at 1 corner st, sc in same st, working in ends of rows, evenly sp 21 sc in ends of rows across, 2 sc in next corner st, sc in each st across to next corner, 2 sc in next corner st, working in ends of rows, evenly sp 21 sc in ends of rows across, 2 sc in next corner st, sc in each st across to first corner, **do not join**. *(124 sc)*

Rnd 2: [Sc in each of next 11 sts, **sc dec** *(see Stitch Guide)* in next 2 sts] 9 times, sc in each of next 5 sts, sc dec in last 2 sts. *(114 sc)*

Rnds 3–11: Sc in each st around. At end of last rnd, **join** *(see Pattern Note)* in beg sc. Fasten off.

SEAT LID COVER
SKILL LEVEL

INTERMEDIATE

FINISHED SIZE

Fits standard round toilet seat lid

MATERIALS

- Medium (worsted) weight yarn:
  5 oz/250 yds/142g variegated blue
  1 oz/50 yds/28g light periwinkle
- Size G/6/4mm crochet hook
  or size needed to obtain gauge
- Tapestry needle
- Narrow white elastic: 1 yd

4 MEDIUM

GAUGE

4 dc = 1 inch; 2 dc rows = 1 inch

PATTERN NOTES

Chain-3 at beginning of row or round counts as first double crochet unless otherwise stated.

Join with slip stitch as indicated unless otherwise stated.

SPECIAL STITCH

Knot stitch (knot st): Tr in next st, sc in next st.

INSTRUCTIONS
COVER

Rnd 1: With variegated blue, ch 4, sl st in first ch to form ring, **ch 3** *(see Pattern Notes)*, 11 dc in ring, join 3rd ch of beg ch 3. *(12 dc)*

Rnd 2: Ch 3, 2 dc in each st around, dc in same st as joining sl st of last rnd, join in 3rd ch of beg ch-3. *(24 dc)*

Rnd 3: Ch 3, dc in next st, [2 dc in next st, dc in next st] around, dc in same st as joining sl st of last rnd, join in 3rd ch of beg ch-3. *(36 dc)*

Rnd 4: Ch 3, dc in next 2 sts, [2 dc in next st, dc in each of next 2 sts] around, dc in same st as joining sl st of last rnd, join in 3rd ch of beg ch-3. *(48 dc)*

Rnd 5: Ch 3, dc in each of next 3 sts, [2 dc in next st, dc in each of next 3 sts] around, dc in same st as joining sl st of last rnd, join in 3rd ch of beg ch-3. *(60 dc)*

Rnd 6: Ch 3, dc in each of next 4 sts, [2 dc in next st, dc in each of next 4 sts] around, dc in same st as joining sl st of last rnd join in 3rd ch of beg ch-3. *(72 dc)*

Rnd 7: Ch 3, dc in each of next 5 sts, [2 dc in next st, dc in each of next 5 sts] around, dc in same st as joining sl st of last rnd, join in 3rd ch of beg ch-3. *(84 dc)*

Rnd 8: Ch 3, dc in each of next 6 sts, [2 dc in next st, dc in each of next 6 sts] around, dc in same st as joining sl st of last rnd, join in 3rd ch of beg ch-3. *(96 dc)*

Rnd 9: Ch 3, dc in each of next 7 sts, [2 dc in next st, dc in each of next 7 sts] around, dc in same st as joining sl st of last rnd, join in 3rd ch of beg ch-3. *(108 dc)*

Rnd 10: Working in **back lps** *(see Stitch Guide)*, ch 3, dc in each of next 5 sts, [2 dc in next st, dc in each of next 5 sts] around, dc in same st as joining sl st of last rnd, join in 3rd ch of beg ch-3. *(126 dc)*

Rnds 11 & 12: Rep rnds 8 and 9. At end of last rnd, fasten off. *(162 dc at end of last rnd)*

Rnd 13: With WS facing, join light periwinkle with sc in first st of last rnd, **knot st** *(see Special Stitch)* around, tr in last st, join in beg sc.

Tr should bend toward the RS of the work.

Rnd 14: Ch 1, sc in first st, knot st around, tr in last st, join in beg sc. Fasten off.

Turn back to RS of work.

Rnd 15: With RS facing, join variegated blue in first st of last rnd, ch 3, dc in each st around, join in 3rd ch of beg ch-3.

Rnd 16: Ch 3, dc in each of next 8 sts, [2 dc in next st, dc in each of next 8 sts] around, dc in same st as joining sl st of last rnd, join in 3rd ch of beg ch-3. *(180 dc)*

Rnds 17 & 18: Ch 3, dc in each st around, join in 3rd ch of beg ch-3.

Rnd 19: Ch 4, sk next st, [dc in next st, ch 1, sk next st] around, join with sl st in 3rd ch of beg ch-4. Fasten off.

CENTER RIDGE
With outer edge of Cover pointing facing, working in rem lps of rnd 9, join light periwinkle with sc in any st, knot st around, tr in last st, join in beg sc. Fasten off.

FINISHING
Weave elastic through sts of rnd 19; sew or tie ends tog.

RUG
SKILL LEVEL
■■■□ INTERMEDIATE

FINISHED SIZE
25 inches across

MATERIALS
- Medium (worsted) weight yarn:
  8 oz/400 yds/227g variegated blue
  4 oz/200 yds/113g light periwinkle
  4 MEDIUM
- Size G/6/4mm crochet hook
  or size needed to obtain gauge

GAUGE
4 dc = 1 inch; 2 dc rows = 1 inch

PATTERN NOTES
Use rug backing on back of rugs that are placed on floors other than carpet.

Chain-3 at beginning of row or round counts as first double crochet unless otherwise stated.

Join with slip stitch as indicated unless otherwise stated.

SPECIAL STITCH
Knot stitch (knot st): Tr in next st, sc in next st.

INSTRUCTIONS
RUG
Rnd 1: With variegated blue, ch 4, sl st in first ch to form ring, **ch 3** *(see Pattern Notes)*, 11 dc in ring, **join** *(see Pattern Notes)* in 3rd ch of beg ch-3. *(12 dc)*

Rnd 2: Ch 3, 2 dc in each st around, dc in same st as joining sl st of last rnd, join in 3rd ch of beg ch-3. *(24 dc)*

Rnd 3: Ch 3, dc in next st, [2 dc in next st, dc in next st] around, dc in same st as joining sl st of last rnd, join in 3rd ch of beg ch-3. *(36 dc)*

Rnd 4: Ch 3, dc in each of next 2 sts, [2 dc in next st, dc in each of next 2 sts] around, dc in same st as joining sl st of last rnd, join in 3rd ch of beg ch-3. *(48 dc)*

Rnd 5: Ch 3, dc in each of next 3 sts, [2 dc in next st, dc in each of next 3 sts] around, dc in same st as joining sl st of last rnd, join in 3rd ch of beg ch-3. *(60 dc)*

Rnd 6: Ch 3, dc in each of next 4 sts, [2 dc in next st, dc in each of next 4 sts] around, dc in same st as joining sl st of last rnd, join in 3rd ch of beg ch-3. *(72 dc)*

Rnd 7: Ch 3, dc in each of next 5 sts, [2 dc in next st, dc in each of next 5 sts] around, dc in same st as joining sl st of last rnd, join in 3rd ch of beg ch-3. *(84 dc)*

Rnd 8: Ch 3, dc in each of next 6 sts, [2 dc in next st, dc in each of next 6 sts] around, dc in same st as joining sl st of last rnd, join in 3rd ch of beg ch-3. *(96 dc)*

Rnd 9: Ch 3, dc in each of next 7 sts, [2 dc in next st, dc in each of next 7 sts] around, dc in same st as joining sl st of last rnd, join in 3rd ch of beg ch-3. *(108 dc)*

Rnd 10: Working in **back lps** *(see Stitch Guide)*, ch 3, dc in each of next 8 sts, [2 dc in next st, dc in each of next 8 sts] around, dc in same st as joining sl st of last rnd, join in 3rd ch of beg ch-3. *(120 dc)*

Rnd 11: Ch 3, dc in each of next 9 sts, [2 dc in next st, dc in each of next 9 sts] around, dc in same st as joining sl st of last rnd, join in 3rd ch of beg ch-3. *(132 dc)*

Rnd 12: Ch 3, dc in each of next 10 sts, [2 dc in next st, dc in each of next 10 sts] around, dc in same st as joining sl st of last rnd, join in 3rd ch of beg ch-3. Fasten off. *(144 dc)*

Rnd 13: With WS facing, join light periwinkle with sc in first st of last rnd, **knot st** *(see Special Stitch)* around, tr in last st, join in beg sc.

Tr should bend toward the RS of work.

Rnd 14: Ch 1, sc in first st, knot st around, tr in last st, join in beg sc. Fasten off.

Turn back to RS of work.

Rnd 15: Join variegated blue in first st of last rnd, ch 3, dc in each of next 11 sts, [2 dc in next st, dc in each of next 11 sts] around, dc in same st as joining sl st of last rnd, join in 3rd ch of beg ch-3. *(156 dc)*

Rnd 16: Ch 3, dc in each of next 12 sts, [2 dc in next st, dc in each of next 12 sts] around, dc in same st as joining sl st of last rnd, join in 3rd ch of beg ch-3. *(168 dc)*

Rnd 17: Ch 3, dc in each of next 13 sts, [2 dc in next st, dc in each of next 13 sts] around, dc in same st as joining sl st of last rnd, join in 3rd ch of beg ch-3. *(180 dc)*

Rnd 18: Ch 3, dc in each of next 14 sts, [2 dc in next st, dc in each of next 14 sts] around, dc in same st as joining sl st of last rnd, join in 3rd ch of beg ch-3. Fasten off. *(192 dc)*

Rnds 19 & 20: Rep rnds 13 and 14.

Rnd 21: Join variegated blue in first st of last rnd, ch 3, dc in each of next 15 sts, [2 dc in next st, dc in each of next 15 sts] around, dc in same st as joining sl st of last rnd, join in 3rd ch of beg ch-3. *(204 dc)*

Rnd 22: Ch 3, dc in each of next 16 sts, [2 dc in next st, dc in each of next 16 sts] around, dc in same st as joining sl st of last rnd, join in 3rd ch of beg ch-3. *(216 dc)*

Rnd 23: Ch 3, dc in each of next 17 sts, [2 dc in next st, dc in each of next 17 sts] around, dc in same st as joining sl st of last rnd, join in 3rd ch of beg ch-3. *(228 dc)*

Rnd 24: Ch 3, dc in each of next 18 sts, [2 dc in next st, dc in each of next 18 sts] around, dc in same st as joining sl st of last rnd, join in 3rd ch of beg ch-3. *(240 dc)*

Rnd 25: Ch 3, dc in each of next 19 sts, [2 dc in next st, dc in each of next 19 sts] around, dc in same st as joining sl st of last rnd, join in 3rd ch of beg ch-3. Fasten off. *(252 dc)*

Rnds 26 & 27: Rep rnds 13 and 14.

CENTER RIDGE

With outer edge of Rug pointing toward you, working in rem lps of rnd 9, join light periwinkle with sc in any st, tr in next st, knot st around, tr in last st, join in beg sc. Fasten off.

TISSUE ROLL COVER
SKILL LEVEL

INTERMEDIATE

FINISHED SIZE
Fits standard-size roll of bath tissue

MATERIALS
- Medium (worsted) weight yarn:
  2 oz/100 yds/57g variegated blue
  ½ oz/25 yds/14g light periwinkle
- Size G/6/4mm crochet hook
  or size needed to obtain gauge

4 MEDIUM

GAUGE
4 sc = 1 inch; 4 sc rows = 1 inch

PATTERN NOTE
Join with slip stitch as indicated unless otherwise stated.

SPECIAL STITCH
Knot stitch (knot st): Tr in next st, sc in next st.

INSTRUCTIONS
COVER
Rnd 1: With variegated blue, ch 4, sl st in first ch to form ring, ch 1, 10 sc in ring, **join** *(see Pattern Note)* in beg sc. *(10 sc)*

Rnd 2: Ch 1, 2 sc in each st around, join in beg sc. *(20 sc)*

Rnd 3: Ch 1, sc in first st, 2 sc in next st, [sc in next st, 2 sc in next st] around, join in beg sc. *(30 sc)*

Rnd 4: Ch 1, sc in each st around, join in beg sc.

Rnd 5: Ch 1, sc in each of first 2 sts, 2 sc in next st, [sc in each of next 2 sts, 2 sc in next st] around, join in beg sc. *(40 sc)*

Rnds 6 & 7: Ch 1, sc in each st around, join in beg sc.

Rnd 8: Ch 1, sc in each of first 3 sts, 2 sc in next st, [sc in each of next 3 sts, 2 sc in next st) around, join in beg sc. *(50 sc)*

Rnd 9: Ch 1, sc in each st around, join in beg sc. Fasten off.

Rnd 10: With WS facing, join light periwinkle with sc in first st of last rnd, **knot st** *(see Special Stitch)* around, tr in last st, join with sl st in beg sc.

Tr should bend toward the RS of work.

Rnd 11: Ch 1, sc in first st, knot st around, tr in last st, join in beg sc. Fasten off.

Turn to RS of work.

Rnd 12: Join variegated blue in first st of last rnd, ch 1, sc in each st around, join in beg sc.

Rnds 13–29: Ch 1, sc in each st around, join. At end of last rnd, fasten off.

Rnds 30 & 31: Rep rnds 10 and 11. ■

Green Retreat
Bath Set AN ORIGINAL BY **ANNIE**

OVAL RUG
SKILL LEVEL

◼◼◼☐
INTERMEDIATE

FINISHED SIZE
27½ x 43 inches

MATERIALS
- Light (sport) weight yarn:
  4 oz/360 yds/113g off-white
- Medium (worsted) weight yarn:
  30 oz/1,500 yds/851g green
- Sizes G/6/4mm and H/8/5mm
  crochet hooks or sizes needed to
  obtain gauge
- Tapestry needle

3
LIGHT

4
MEDIUM

GAUGE
Size G hook: 4 hdc = 1 inch

Size H hook: 7 hdc = 2 inches; 5 hdc rows =
2 inches

PATTERN NOTES
Use size H hook unless otherwise stated.

Chain-2 at beginning of row or round
counts as first half double crochet unless
otherwise stated.

Join with slip stitch as indicated unless
otherwise stated.

Chain-3 at beginning of row or round counts as
first double crochet unless otherwise stated.

INSTRUCTIONS
RUG
Rnd 1: With **size H hook** (*see Pattern Notes*) and
green, ch 46, working in **back bar of ch** (*see Fig.
1*), 4 hdc in 3rd ch from hook (*first 2 chs count*
as first hdc), hdc in each ch across to last ch, 5
hdc in last ch, working on opposite side of ch
in **back lps** (*see Stitch Guide*), hdc in each ch
across, **join** (*see Pattern Notes*) in 2nd ch of beg
ch-2. (*94 hdc*)

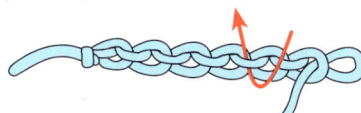

Fig. 1
Back Bar of Chain

Rnd 2: Working this rnd and rem rnds in back
lps, **ch 2** (*see Pattern Notes*), hdc in same st, 2
hdc in each of next 4 sts, hdc in each of next 42
sts, 2 hdc in each of next 5 sts, hdc in each of
last 42 sts, join in 2nd ch of beg ch-2. (*104 hdc*)

Rnd 3: Ch 2, hdc in same st, hdc in next st,
[2 hdc in next st, hdc in next st] 4 times, hdc
in each of next 42 sts, [hdc in next st, 2 hdc in
next st] 5 times, hdc in each of last 42 sts, join
in 2nd ch of beg ch-2. (*114 hdc*)

Rnd 4: Ch 2, hdc in next st, 2 hdc in next st, [hdc
in each of next 2 sts, 2 hdc in next st] 4 times,
hdc in each of next 42 sts, [2 hdc in next st, hdc
in each of next 2 sts] 5 times, hdc in each of last
42 sts, join in 2nd ch of beg ch-2. (*124 hdc*)

Rnd 5: Ch 2, hdc in same st, hdc in each of
next 3 sts, [2 hdc in next st, hdc in each of next
3 sts] 4 times, hdc in each of next 42 sts, [hdc
in each of next 3 sts, 2 hdc in next st] 5 times,
hdc in each of last 42 sts, join in 2nd ch of beg
ch-2. (*134 hdc*)

Rnd 6: Ch 2, hdc in each of next 3 sts, 2 hdc in
next st, [hdc in each of next 4 sts, 2 hdc in next
st] 4 times, hdc in each of next 42 sts, [2 hdc
in next st, hdc in each of next 4 sts] 5 times,
hdc in each of last 42 sts, join in 2nd ch of beg
ch-2. (*144 hdc*)

Rnd 7: Ch 2, hdc in same st, hdc in each of next 5 sts, [2 hdc in next st, hdc in each of next 5 sts] 4 times, hdc in each of next 42 sts, [hdc in each of next 5 sts, 2 hdc in next st] 5 times, hdc in each of last 42 sts, join in 2nd ch of beg ch-2. *(154 hdc)*

Rnd 8: Ch 2, hdc in each of next 5 sts, 2 hdc in next st, [hdc in each of next 6 sts, 2 hdc in next st] 4 times, hdc in each of next 42 sts, [2 hdc in next st, hdc in each of next 6 sts] 5 times, hdc in each of last 42 sts, join in 2nd ch of beg ch-2. *(164 hdc)*

Rnd 9: Ch 2, hdc in each of next 3 sts, [2 hdc in next st, hdc in each of next 7 sts] 5 times, hdc in each of next 42 sts, [hdc in each of next 7 sts, 2 hdc in next st] 5 times, hdc in each of last 38 sts, join in 2nd ch of beg ch-2. *(174 hdc)*

Rnd 10: Ch 2, hdc in each of next 3 sts, [hdc in each of next 8 sts, 2 hdc in next st] 5 times, hdc in each of next 42 sts, [2 hdc in next st, hdc in each of next 8 sts] 5 times, hdc in each of last 38 sts, join in 2nd ch of beg ch-2. *(184 hdc)*

Rnd 11: Ch 2, hdc in each of next 3 sts, [2 hdc in next st, hdc in each of next 9 sts] 5 times, hdc in each of next 42 sts, [hdc in each of next 9 sts, 2 hdc in next st] 5 times, hdc in each of last 38 sts, join in 2nd ch of beg ch-2. *(194 hdc)*

Rnd 12: Ch 2, hdc in each of next 3 sts, [hdc in each of next 10 sts, 2 hdc in next st] 5 times, hdc in each of next 42 sts, [2 hdc in next st, hdc in each of next 10 sts] 5 times, hdc in each of last 38 sts, join in 2nd ch of beg ch-2. *(204 hdc)*

Rnd 13: Ch 2, hdc in each of next 3 sts, [2 hdc in next st, hdc in each of next 11 sts] 5 times, hdc in each of next 42 sts, [hdc in each of next 11 sts, 2 hdc in next st] 5 times, hdc in each of last 38 sts, join in 2nd ch of beg ch-2. *(214 hdc)*

Rnd 14: Ch 2, hdc in each of next 3 sts, [hdc in each of next 12 sts, 2 hdc in next st] 5 times, hdc in each of next 42 sts, [2 hdc in next st, hdc in each of next 12 sts] 5 times, hdc in each of last 38 sts, join in 2nd ch of beg ch-2. *(224 hdc)*

Rnd 15: Ch 2, hdc in each of next 7 sts, [2 hdc in next st, hdc in each of next 13 sts] 5 times, hdc in each of next 42 sts, [hdc in each of next 13 sts, 2 hdc in next st] 5 times, hdc in each of last 34 sts, join in 2nd ch of beg ch-2. *(234 hdc)*

Rnd 16: Ch 2, hdc in each of next 7 sts, [hdc in each of next 14 sts, 2 hdc in next st] 5 times, hdc in each of next 42 sts, [2 hdc in next st, hdc in each of next 14 sts] 5 times, hdc in each of last 34 sts, join in 2nd ch of beg ch-2. *(244 hdc)*

Rnd 17: Ch 2, hdc in each of next 7 sts, [2 hdc in next st, hdc in each of next 15 sts] 5 times, hdc in each of next 42 sts, [hdc in each of next 15 sts, 2 hdc in next st] 5 times, hdc in each of last 34 sts join in 2nd ch of beg ch-2. *(254 hdc)*

Rnd 18: Ch 2, hdc in each of next 7 sts, [hdc in each of next 16 sts, 2 hdc in next st] 5 times, hdc in each of next 42 sts, [2 hdc in next st, hdc in each of next 16 sts] 5 times, hdc in each of last 34 sts, join in 2nd ch of beg ch-2. *(264 hdc)*

Rnd 19: Ch 2, hdc in each of next 9 sts, [2 hdc in next st, hdc in each of next 20 sts] 4 times, hdc in each of next 48 sts, [hdc in each of next 20 sts, 2 hdc in next st] 4 times, hdc in each of last 38 sts, join in 2nd ch of beg ch-2. *(272 hdc)*

Rnd 20: Ch 2, hdc in each of next 9 sts, [hdc in each of next 21 sts, 2 hdc in next st] 4 times, hdc in each of next 48 sts, [2 hdc in next st, hdc in each of next 21 sts] 4 times, hdc in each of last 38 sts, join in 2nd ch of beg ch-2. *(280 hdc)*

Rnd 21: Ch 2, hdc in each of next 9 sts, [2 hdc in next st, hdc in each of next 22 sts] 4 times, hdc in each of next 48 sts, [hdc in each of next 22 sts, 2 hdc in next st] 4 times, hdc in each of last 38 sts, join in 2nd ch of beg ch-2. Fasten off. *(288 hdc)*

CHAIN LOOPS

Starting at center of rnd 1 and working in rem lps, join green with sc in lp at end of rnd 1 opposite of joining sl st, [ch 7, sc in next lp] across, *ch 1, sc in first lp of next rnd, [ch 7, sc in next lp] around, rep from * to last rnd, join in beg sc on last rnd of Chain Loops. Leaving both lps of last rnd unworked, fasten off.

LACE

Rnd 1: With RS of Rug facing, working in both lps of last rnd on Rug, join off-white in 13th st from joining at end of rnd, **ch 3** (*see Pattern Notes*), dc in each of next 46 sts, [2 dc in next st, dc in each of next 20 sts] 3 times, 2 dc in next st, dc in each of next 82 sts, [2 dc in next st, dc in each of next 20 sts] 3 times, 2 dc in next st, dc in each of last 31 sts, join in 3rd ch of beg ch-3. (*296 dc*)

Rnd 2: Ch 1, sc in each of first 2 sts, ch 3, sk next 2 sts, [sc in each of next 2 sts, ch 3, sk next 2 sts] around, join in beg sc. (*148 sc, 74 ch sps*)

Rnd 3: Ch 3, dc in next st, ch 3, sk next ch sp, [dc in each of next 2 sts, ch 3, sk next ch sp] around, join in 3rd ch of beg ch-3.

Rnd 4: Ch 1, sc in sp between ch 3 and next dc, ch 4, sk next ch sp, [sc in sp between next 2 dc, ch 4, sk next ch sp] around, join in beg sc. (*74 sc, 74 ch sps*)

Rnd 5: Ch 1, sc in first st, 5 sc in next ch sp, [sc in next st, 5 sc in next ch sp] around, join in beg sc. (*444 sc*)

Rnd 6: Ch 1, sc in first st, ch 1, sk next 2 sts, (dc, ch 2, dc) in next st, ch 1, sk next 2 sts, *sc in next st, ch 1, sk next 2 sts, (dc, ch 2, dc) in next st, ch 1, sk next 2 sts, rep from * around, join in beg sc. (*74 sc, 74 ch sps*)

Rnd 7: Ch 1, sc in first sc, 6 dc in next ch-2 sp, [sc in next st, 6 sc in next ch-2 sp] around, join in beg sc. Fasten off.

RIBBON

With size G hook and green, ch 396, working in back bar of ch, hdc in 3rd ch from hook, hdc in each ch across. Fasten off.

Weave under and over 2 dc at a time through sps of rnd 3 on Lace.

Sew ends tog. Hide seam on WS of Lace.

BOW
MAKE 2.

With size G hook and green, ch 53, working in back bar of ch, hdc in 3rd ch from hook, hdc in each ch across. Fasten off.

Fold according to diagram (*see Fig. 2*).

Fig. 2
Oval Rug
Bow Folding Diagram

Tie 6-inch piece green in knot around center of folded bow.

CENTER LOOP

With size G hook and green, ch 9, working in back bar of ch, hdc in 3rd ch from hook, hdc in each ch across. Fasten off.

Wrap Center Loop around center of Bow, sew ends tog.

Sew 1 Bow to ribbon at each end of Rug.

LID COVER
SKILL LEVEL

INTERMEDIATE

FINISHED SIZE
Fits standard or oval toilet lid

MATERIALS
- Medium (worsted) weight yarn: 14 oz/700 yds/397g green
- Size H/8/5mm crochet hook or size needed to obtain gauge
- Tapestry needle
- Sewing needle
- Sewing thread
- ⅛-inch-wide elastic: 1 yd

4 MEDIUM

GAUGE
7 hdc = 2 inches; 5 hdc rows = 2 inches

PATTERN NOTES
Chain-2 at beginning of row or round counts as first half double crochet unless otherwise stated.

Work all rows beginning with row 2 alternating front and back loops. All unworked loops should be on same side of piece.

Join with slip stitch as indicated unless otherwise stated.

INSTRUCTIONS
COVER

Row 1: Ch 28, working in **back bar of ch** (see Fig. 1), hdc in 3rd ch from hook (first 2 chs count as first hdc), hdc in each ch across to last ch, 5 hdc in last ch, working on opposite side of ch in **back lps** (see Stitch Guide), hdc in each ch across with last st in bottom of ch 2, turn. (57 hdc)

Fig. 1
Back Bar of Chain

Row 2: Working this row in **front lps** (see Stitch Guide and Pattern Notes), **ch 2** (see Pattern Notes), hdc in each of next 25 sts, 2 hdc in each of next 5 sts, hdc in each of last 26 sts, turn. (62 hdc)

Row 3: Working this row in back lps, ch 2, hdc in each of next 25 sts, [2 hdc in next st, hdc in next st] 5 times, hdc in each of last 26 sts, turn. (67 hdc)

Row 4: Ch 2, hdc in each of next 25 sts, [2 hdc in next st, hdc in each of each of next 2 sts] 5 times, hdc in each of last 26 sts, turn. (72 hdc)

Row 5: Ch 2, hdc in each of next 25 sts, [2 hdc in next st, hdc in each of next 3 sts] 5 times, hdc in each of last 26 sts, turn. (77 hdc)

Row 6: Ch 2, hdc in each of next 25 sts, [2 hdc in next st, hdc in each of next 4 sts] 5 times, hdc in each of next 26 sts, turn. (82 hdc)

Row 7: Ch 2, hdc in each of next 25 sts, [2 hdc in next st, hdc in each of next 5 sts] 5 times, hdc in each of last 26 sts, turn. (87 hdc)

Row 8: Ch 2, hdc in each of next 25 sts, [2 hdc in next st, hdc in each of next 6 sts] 5 times, hdc in each of last 26 sts, turn. (92 hdc)

Row 9: Ch 1, sc in first st, hdc in each of next 25 sts, [2 hdc in next st, hdc in each of next 7 sts] 5 times, hdc in each of next 25 sts, sc in last st, turn. (95 hdc, 2 sc)

Row 10: Sl st in each of first 2 sts, sc in next st, hdc in each of next 23 sts, [2 hdc in next st, hdc in each of ... of ... ving ... ts)

... sts, ... hdc in ... hdc in ... xt st ... 2 sc,

... ts, ... lc in ... hdc ... ext ... ; 2

Row 13: Sk first sl st, sl st in each of next 3 sts, sc in next st, hdc in each of next 32 sts, 2 hdc in next st, [hdc in each of next 12 sts, 2 hdc in next st] twice, hdc in each of next 31 sts, sc in next st, sl st in next st leaving last 5 sts unworked, turn. (93 hdc, 2 sc, 4 sl sts)

Row 14: Sk first sl st, sl st in each of next 3 sts, sc in next st, hdc in each of next 32 sts, 2 hdc in next st, [hdc in each of next 10 sts, 2 hdc in next st] twice, hdc in each of next 32 sts, sc in next st, sl st in next st leaving last 5 sts unworked, turn. *(90 hdc, 2 sc, 4 sl sts)*

Row 15: Sk first sl st, sl st in each of next 3 sts, sc in next st, hdc in each of next 31 sts, 2 hdc in next st, [hdc in each of next 9 sts, 2 hdc in next st] twice, hdc in each of next 32 sts, sc in next st, sl st in next st leaving last 5 sts unworked, turn. Fasten off. *(87 hdc, 2 sc, 4 sl sts)*

Rnd 16: Now working in rnds, around outer edge, join with sc in end of row 9 at right back corner, sc in end of each row and in each st around, **join** *(see Pattern Notes)* in beg sc. *(139 sc)*

Rnd 17: Ch 1, sc in each st around, join in beg sc, **turn.**

Row 18: Working in rows through both lps of sts, ch 1, sc in each of first 121 sts leaving last 18 sts unworked, turn. *(121 sc)*

Row 19: Ch 1, sc in each of first 23 sts, **sc dec** *(see Stitch Guide)* in next 2 sts, [sc in each of next 16 sts, sc dec in next 2 sts] 4 times, sc in each of last 24 sts, turn. *(116 sc)*

Row 20: Leaving excess extended at each end, hold elastic over sts of last row, **working over elastic** *(see Fig. 2)*, ch 1, sc in each st across. Fasten off.

Fig. 2
Single Crochet Around Elastic Into Stitches

TIE
Join in 1 end of row 20, ch 43, sl st in 2nd ch from hook and in each ch across, join in same row. Fasten off.

Rep on opposite end of row 20.

CHAIN LOOPS
Starting at center of row 1 and working in rem lps, join green with sc in lp at rounded end, [ch 7, sc in next lp] across, *ch 1, sc in first lp of next rnd, [ch 7, sc in next lp] across, rep from * to last row. Leaving both lps of last rnd unworked, fasten off.

FINISHING
Place Cover on lid of toilet, pull ends of elastic, gathering edge of cover to fit lid. Leaving ¾-inch end, cut off excess ends. Fold each end under, sew to back of last row on Cover to secure.

TANK LID COVER
SKILL LEVEL
INTERMEDIATE

FINISHED SIZE
Fits standard tank lid

MATERIALS
- Light (sport) weight yarn: 3 oz/270 yds/85g off-white
- Medium (worsted) weight yarn: 7 oz/350 yds/199g green
- Sizes G/6/4mm and H/8/5mm crochet hooks or sizes needed to obtain gauge
- Tapestry needle

3 LIGHT
4 MEDIUM

GAUGE
Size G hook: 4 hdc = 1 inch

Size H hook: 7 hdc = 2 inches; 5 hdc rows = 2 inches

PATTERN NOTES

Use size H hook unless otherwise stated.

Chain-2 at beginning of row or round
counts as first half double crochet unless
otherwise stated.

Join with slip stitch as indicated unless
otherwise stated.

Chain-3 at beginning of row or round counts as
first double crochet unless otherwise stated.

SPECIAL STITCH

Slanted V-stitch (slanted V-st): (Sc, ch 1, dc)
as indicated.

INSTRUCTIONS
COVER

Row 1: With **size H hook** (*see Pattern Notes*) and
green, ch 80, **slanted V-st** (*see Special Stitch*) in
2nd ch from hook, [sk next 2 chs, slanted V-st
in next ch] across, turn. (*27 slanted V-sts*)

Rows 2–20: Ch 1, slanted V-st in each ch-1 sp
across, turn. At end of last row, **do not turn.**

Rnd 21: Now working in rnds, ch 1, [2 sc in end
of next row, hdc in ch-1 sp of slanted V-st at end
of next row] 10 times, working in starting ch on
opposite side of row 1, 2 sc in first ch, sc in each
ch across, [2 sc in end of next row, hdc in ch-1
sp of slanted V-st at end of next row] 10 times,
sc in each st and in each ch-1 sp across to last st,
sk last st, **join** (*see Pattern Notes*) in **back lp** (*see
Stitch Guide*) of first sc. (*219 sc*)

Rnd 22: Working this rnd in back lps, ch 1, sc in
each st around, join in beg sc.

Rnd 23: Ch 1, slanted V-st in same st as ch 1, sk
next 2 sts, [slanted V-st in next st, sk next 2 sts]
around, join in beg sc, **turn.** (*73 slanted V-sts*)

Rnds 24–28: Ch 1, slanted V-st in each ch-1 sp
around, join in beg sc, turn. At end of last rnd,
fasten off.

LACE

Rnd 1: Working in rem lps of rnd 21 on Cover,
with size G hook, join off-white with sc in first

st, sc in each st around with 2 sc in last st, join
in back lp of beg sc. (*220 sc*)

Rnd 2: Working this rnd in back lps, ch 1, sc in
each of first 2 sts, ch 2, sk next 2 sts, [sc in each
of next 2 sts, ch 2 sk next 2 sts] around, join in
beg sc. (*110 sc, 55 ch sps*)

Rnd 3: **Ch 3** (*see Pattern Notes*), dc in next st,
ch 2, sk next ch sp, [dc in each of next 2 sts,
ch2, sk next ch sp] around, join in 3rd ch of
beg ch-3. (*110 dc, 55 ch sps*)

Rnd 4: Ch 1, sc in sp between ch 3 and next dc,
ch 3, sk next ch sp, [sc in sp between next 2 dc,
ch 3, sk next ch sp] around, join in beg sc. (*55
sc, 55 ch sps*)

Rnd 5: Ch 1, sc in first st, 2 sc in next ch sp, [sc
in next st, 2 sc in next ch sp] around, join in beg
sc. (*165 sc*)

Rnd 6: Ch 1, sc in first st, ch 1, sk next 2 sts, (dc,
ch 2, dc) in next st, *ch 1, sk next 2 sts, sc in
next st, ch 1, sk next 2 sts, (dc, ch 2, dc) in next
st, rep from * around to last 5 sts, ch 1, sk next
st, sc in next st, ch 1, sk next st, (dc, ch 2, dc) in
next st, ch 1, sk last st, join in beg sc.

Rnd 7: Ch 1, sc in first sc, 6 dc in next ch-2 sp,
[sc in next st, 6 sc in next ch-2 sp] around, join
in beg sc. Fasten off.

TRIM

With top of piece facing, working in front lps of
rnd 1 on Lace, join off-white in any st, 3 sc in
next st, [sl st in next st, 3 sc in next st] around,
join beg sl st. Fasten off.

RIBBON

With size G hook and green, ch 240, working in
back bar of ch (*see Fig. 1*), hdc in 3rd ch from
hook, hdc in each ch across. Fasten off.

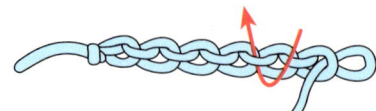

Fig. 1
Back Bar of Chain

Beg at center back, weave under and over
2 dc at a time through sps of rnd 3 on Lace.

Sew ends tog. Hide seam behind first 2 dc and last 2 dc of rnd.

TISSUE ROLL COVER
SKILL LEVEL

■■■□
INTERMEDIATE

FINISHED SIZE
Fits 4½-inch-diameter roll of bath tissue

MATERIALS
- Light (sport) weight yarn:
  ½ oz/45 yds/14g off-white
- Medium (worsted) weight yarn:
  2 oz/100 yds/57g green
- Sizes D/3/3.25mm and H/8/5mm crochet hooks or sizes needed to obtain gauge
- Tapestry needle
- Fiberfill

3 LIGHT

4 MEDIUM

GAUGE
Size D hook: 11 sts = 2 inches

Size H hook: 7 hdc = 2 inches; 5 hdc rows = 2 inches

PATTERN NOTES
Use size H hook unless otherwise stated.

Join with slip stitch as indicated unless otherwise stated.

Chain-3 at beginning of row or round counts as first double crochet unless otherwise stated.

SPECIAL STITCH
Slanted V-stitch (slanted V-st): (Sc, ch 1, dc) as indicated.

INSTRUCTIONS
COVER
Rnd 1: With **size H hook** (*see Pattern Notes*) and green, ch 5, 11 tr in 5th ch from hook (*first 4 chs count as first tr*), **join** (*see Pattern Notes*) in 4th ch of beg ch-5. (*12 tr*)

Rnd 2: Ch 1, **sc dec** (*see Stitch Guide*) in first 2 sts, [sc dec in next 2 sts] around, join in beg sc. Stuff with fiberfill.

Rnd 3: **Ch 3** (*see Pattern Notes*), 2 dc in same st, 3 dc in each st around, join in 3rd ch of beg ch-3. (*18 dc*)

Rnd 4: Ch 3, dc in same st, 2 dc in each st around, join in 3rd ch of beg ch-3. (*36 dc*)

Rnd 5: Ch 3, dc in same st, dc in next st, [2 dc in next st, dc in next st] around, join in 3rd ch of beg ch-3. (*54 dc*)

Rnd 6: Working in **back lps** (*see Stitch Guide*), ch 1, sc in each st around, join in beg sc.

Rnd 7: Ch 1, **slanted V-st** (*see Special Stitch*) in first st, sk next 2 sts, [slanted V-st in next st, sk next 2 sts] around, join in beg sc, turn.

Rnds 8–18: Ch 1, slanted V-st in each ch-1 sp around, join in beg sc, turn. At end of last rnd, fasten off.

LACE
Rnd 1: Working in **front lps** (*see Stitch Guide*) of rnd 5 on Cover, with size D hook and off-white, join with sc in first st, sc in same st, 2 sc in each of next 2 sts, [sc in next st, 2 sc in next st] around, 2 sc in each of last 3 sts, join in back lp of beg sc. (*36 sc*)

Rnd 2: Working this rnd in back lps, ch 1, sc in each st around, join with in both lps of beg sc.

Rnd 3: Ch 1, sc in first st, ch 2, sk next 2 sts, [sc in next st, ch 2, sk next 2 sts] around, join in beg sc. *(12 sc, 12 ch sps)*

Rnd 4: Sl st in first ch sp, ch 3, dc in same ch sp, ch 1, sk next st, [2 dc in next ch sp, ch 1, sk next st] around, join in 3rd ch of beg ch-3. *(24 dc, 12 ch sps)*

Rnd 5: Sl st in next st, ch 1, [sc in next ch, ch 3, sk next 2 sts] around, join in beg sc. *(12 sc, 12 ch sps)*

Rnd 6: Ch 1, 3 sc in each ch sp around, join in beg sc. *(36 sc)*

Rnd 7: Ch 1, sc in first st, ch 2, sk next 2 sts, (dc, ch 2, dc) in next st, ch 2, sk next 2 sts, *sc in next st, ch 2, sk next 2 sts, (dc, ch 2, dc) in next st, ch 2, sk next 2 sts, rep from * around, join in beg sc. *(6 sc, 6 ch sps)*

Rnd 8: Ch 1, sc in first sc, sk next ch-2 sp, 9 dc in next ch-2 sp, sk next ch-2 sp, [sc in next sc, sk next ch-2 sp, 9 dc in next ch-2 sp, sk next ch-2 sp] around, join in beg sc. Fasten off.

TRIM

With top of piece facing, working in front lps of rnd 1 on Lace, with size D hook and off-white, join in any st, 4 sc in next st, [sl st in next st, 4 sc in next st] around, join in beg sl st. Fasten off.

BOUTIQUE TISSUE COVER
SKILL LEVEL

INTERMEDIATE

FINISHED SIZE

Fits 4⅜ x 5¼-inch boutique tissue box

MATERIALS

- Light (sport) weight yarn:
  ½ oz/45 yds/14g off-white
- Medium (worsted) weight yarn:
  3 oz/150 yds/85g green
- Sizes D/3/3.25mm and H/8/5mm crochet hooks or sizes needed to obtain gauge
- Tapestry needle

3 LIGHT

4 MEDIUM

GAUGE

Size D hook: 11 sts = 2 inches

Size H hook: 7 sts = 2 inches; 5 rows = 2 inches

PATTERN NOTES

Use size H hook unless otherwise stated.

Join with slip stitch as indicated unless otherwise stated.

Chain-3 at beginning of row or round **does not** count as first double crochet unless otherwise stated.

SPECIAL STITCH

Slanted V-stitch (slanted V-st): (Sc, ch 1, dc) as indicated.

INSTRUCTIONS
COVER

Rnd 1: With **size H hook** *(see Pattern Notes)* and green, ch 28, working in **back bar of ch** *(see Fig. 1)*, sl st in first ch to form ring, ch 1, (sc, ch 1, sc) in same ch, sc in each of next 6 chs, *(sc, ch 1, sc) in next ch, sc in each of next 6 chs, rep from * around, **join** *(see Pattern Notes)* in beg sc. *(32 sc, 4 ch sps)*

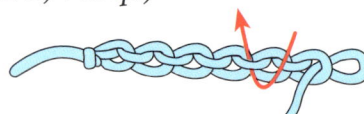

Fig. 1
Back Bar of Chain

Rnd 2: Sl st in first ch sp, ch 3, 2 dc in same ch sp, dc in each of next 8 sts, [3 dc in next ch sp, dc in each of next 8 sts] 3 times, dc in same sp as beg 2 dc, join in top of beg dc. *(44 dc)*

Rnd 3: Ch 3, 3 dc in first st, dc in each of next 10 sts, [5 dc in next st, dc in each of next 10 sts] 3 times, 2 dc in same st as beg 3 dc, join in **back lp** *(see Stitch Guide)* of beg dc. *(60 dc)*

Rnd 4: Working this rnd in back lps, ch 1, sc in each st around, join in beg sc.

Rnd 5: Ch 1, **slanted V-st** *(see Special Stitch)* in first st, sk next 2 sts, [slanted V-st in next st, sk next 2 sts] around, join in beg sc, **turn.**

Rnds 6–19: Ch 1, slanted V-st in each ch-1 sp around, join in beg sc, turn. At end of last rnd, fasten off.

LACE

Rnd 1: Working in **front lps** (*see Stitch Guide*) of rnd 3 on Cover, with size D hook and off-white, join with sc in first st, sc in same st, 2 sc in each of next 2 sts, [sc in next st, 2 sc in next st] around, 2 sc in each of last 3 sts, join in back lp of beg sc. *(36 sc)*

Rnd 2: Working this rnd in back lps, ch 1, sc in each st around, join with in both lps of beg sc.

Rnd 3: Ch 1, sc in first st, ch 2, sk next 2 sts, [sc in next st, ch 2, sk next 2 sts] around, join in beg sc. *(12 sc, 12 ch sps)*

Rnd 4: Sl st in first ch sp, ch 3, dc in same ch sp, ch 1, sk next st, [2 dc in next ch sp, ch 1, sk next st] around, join in 3rd ch of beg ch-3. *(24 dc, 12 ch sps)*

Rnd 5: Sl st in next st, ch 1, [sc in next ch, ch 3, sk next 2 sts] around, join in beg sc. *(12 sc, 12 ch sps)*

Rnd 6: Ch 1, 3 sc in each ch sp around, join in beg sc. *(36 sc)*

Rnd 7: Ch 1, sc in first st, ch 2, sk next 2 sts, (dc, ch 2, dc) in next st, ch 2, sk next 2 sts, *sc in next st, ch 2, sk next 2 sts, (dc, ch 2, dc) in next st, ch 2, sk next 2 sts, rep from * around, join in beg sc. *(6 sc, 6 ch sps)*

Rnd 8: Ch 1, sc in first sc, sk next ch-2 sp, 9 dc in next ch-2 sp, sk next ch-2 sp, [sc in next sc, sk next ch-2 sp, 9 dc in next ch-2 sp, sk next ch-2 sp] around, join in beg sc. Fasten off.

TRIM

With top of piece facing, working in front lps of rnd 1 on Lace, with size D hook and off-white, join in any st, 4 sc in next st, [sl st in next st, 4 sc in next st] around, join in beg sl st. Fasten off. ∎

Desert Spa
Bath Set
AN ORIGINAL BY **ANNIE**

TANK LID COVER
SKILL LEVEL

▰▰▰▱ **INTERMEDIATE**

FINISHED SIZE
9 x 22 inches

MATERIALS
- Medium (worsted) weight yarn:
  2 oz/100 yds/57g buff
  1 oz/50 yds/28g each carrot
  and dark blue
- Size H/8/5mm crochet hook
  or size needed to obtain gauge

4 MEDIUM

GAUGE
10 dc = 3 inches; 5 dc rows = 3 inches

PATTERN NOTES
Single crochet and chain-2 at beginning of row
  or round counts as first double crochet unless
  otherwise stated.

Chain-3 at beginning of row or round **does
  not** count as first double crochet unless
  otherwise stated.

Join with slip stitch as indicated unless
  otherwise stated.

INSTRUCTIONS
COVER
Rnd 1: With buff, ch 45, **sc in 2nd ch from
  hook, ch 2** (*see Pattern Notes*), 3 dc in same
  ch, dc in each of next 42 chs, 4 dc in last ch,
  working on opposite side of ch, dc in each of
  next 42 chs, **join** (*see Pattern Notes*) in 2nd ch
  of beg ch-2. (*92 dc*)

Rnd 2: **Ch 3** (*see Pattern Notes*), 3 dc in same st
  as beg ch-3, hdc in each of next 2 sts, 4 dc in
  next st, dc in each of next 42 sts, 4 dc in next st,
  hdc in each of next 2 sts, 4 dc in next st, dc in
  each of next 42 sts, dc in same st as first 3 dc,
  sk ch-3 and join in top of beg dc. (*104 sts*)

Rnd 3: Ch 3, 2 dc in first st, dc in each of next 5
  sts, 4 dc in next st, dc in each of next 45 sts, 4 dc
  in next st, dc in each of next 5 sts, 4 dc in next st,
  dc in each of next 45 sts, 2 dc in same st as first 2
  dc, sk ch-3 and join in top of beg dc. (*116 sts*)

Rnd 4: Ch 3, 3 dc in first st, dc in each of next
  8 sts, 6 dc in next st, dc in each of next 48 sts,
  6 dc in next st, dc in each of next 8 sts, 6 dc
  in next st, dc in each of next 48 sts, 3 dc in
  same st as beg 3 dc, sk ch-3 and join in top
  of beg dc. (*136 dc*)

Rnd 5: Ch 4 (*does not count as first st*), (tr, 2 dc)
  in same st, *dc in each of next 13 sts, (2 dc, 2 tr,
  2 dc) in next st, dc in each of next 53 sts*,
  (2 dc, 2 tr, 2 dc) in next st, rep between * once,
  (2 dc, tr) in same st as beg tr, join in top of beg
  tr. (*156 sts*)

Rnd 6: Ch 3, 3 dc in first st, *dc in each of next 18 sts, 6 dc in next st, dc in each of next 58 sts*, 6 dc in next st, rep between * once, 3 dc in same st as beg 3 dc, join in top of beg dc. *(176 dc)*

Rnd 7: Ch 3, 3 dc in first st, *dc in each of next 22 sts, 5 dc in next st, dc in each of next 64 sts*, 5 dc in next st, rep between * once, 2 dc in same st as beg 3 dc, join in top of beg dc. Fasten off.

Rnd 8: Join carrot with sc in any center corner st, sc in each st around, join in beg sc. Fasten off.

Rnd 9: Join blue in first st, ch 1, working from left to right, **reverse sc** *(see Fig. 1)* in next st, reverse sc in each st around, join in beg reverse sc. Fasten off.

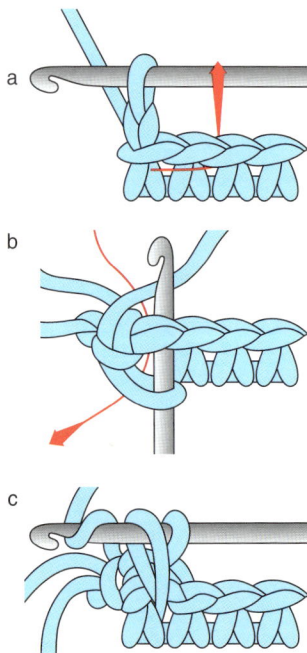

Fig. 1
Reverse Single Crochet

SEAT LID COVER
SKILL LEVEL

INTERMEDIATE

FINISHED SIZE
Instructions given are for 14½ x 16-inch lid cover; changes for 14½ x 18½-inch lid cover are in [ ].

MATERIALS
- Medium (worsted) weight yarn:
  4 oz/200 yds/113g off-white
  2 oz/100 yds/57g buff
  1 oz/50 yds/28g each carrot, light coral, dark blue and country blue
- Size H/8/5mm crochet hook or size needed to obtain gauge
- Sewing needle
- White sewing thread
- ⅛-inch-wide white elastic: 1 yd

GAUGE
10 dc = 3 inches; 5 dc rows = 3 inches

PATTERN NOTES
Single crochet and chain-2 at beginning of row or round counts as first double crochet unless otherwise stated.

Chain-3 at beginning of row or round **does not** count as first double crochet unless otherwise stated.

Join with slip stitch as indicated unless otherwise stated.

INSTRUCTIONS
COVER
CENTER STRIPE
Row 1: With buff, ch 49, working in **back bar of ch** *(see Fig. 1)*, **sc in 2nd ch from hook, ch 2** *(see Pattern Notes)*, dc in each ch across, **do not turn**. Fasten off. *(48 dc)*

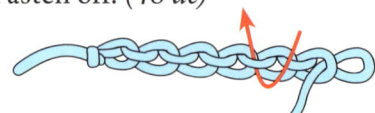

Fig. 1
Back Bar of Chain

Row 2: Join buff with sc in first st, sc in each st across, **do not turn**. Fasten off.

Row 3: Join carrot with sc in first st, ch 3, tr in next st, [ch 1, sk next st, tr in each of next 2 sts] across to last st, sk last st, **do not turn**. Fasten off.

Row 4: Join buff with sc in first st, sc in next st, working in front of ch-1, tr in sk st on row before last, [sc in each of next 2 sts, working in front of ch-1, tr in sk st on row before last] across, **do not turn**. Fasten off.

Row 5: Join buff with sc in first st, ch 2, dc in each st across, **do not turn**. Fasten off.

BACK SECTION
Row 6: Join light coral with **fpsc** *(see Stitch Guide)* around first dc on last row, ch 2, **bpdc** *(see Stitch Guide)* around each st across, **do not turn**. Fasten off.

Row 7: With dark blue, rep row 6.

Row 8: With country blue, rep row 6.

Row 9: With carrot, rep row 6.

Row 10: Join off-white with fpsc around first dc on last row, ch 2, bpdc around each st across, turn. **Do not fasten off.**

18½-INCH SIZE ONLY
Rows [11 & 12]: Ch 1, sc in first st, ch 2, dc in each st across, turn.

FOR BOTH SIZES
Row 11 [13]: Ch 1, sc in first st, ch 2, [**dc dec** *(see Stitch Guide)* in next 2 sts] twice, dc in each st across to last 4 sts, [dc dec in next 2 sts] twice, turn. *(44 dc)*

Row 12 [14]: Ch 1, sc in first st, ch 2, dc dec in next 2 sts, dc in each st across to last 2 sts, dc dec in last 2 sts, turn. *(42 dc)*

Rows 13–18 [15–20]: *Rep rows 11 and 12 [13 and 14] alternately, rep from * 1 [2] times. At end of last row, fasten off. *(24 sts at end of last row)*

FRONT SECTION
Row 19 [21]: Working in starting ch on opposite side of row 1, join light coral with fpsc around first dc, ch 2, bpdc around each st across, **do not turn**. Fasten off.

Rows 20–23 [22–25]: Rep rows 7–10 of Back Section.

18½-INCH SIZE ONLY
Rows [26 & 27]: Ch 1, sc in first st, ch 2, dc in each st across, turn.

FOR BOTH SIZES
Row 24 [28]: Ch 1, sc in first st, ch 2, [dc dec in next 2 sts] twice, dc in each st across to last 4 sts, [dc dec in next 2 sts] twice, turn. *(44 dc)*

Row 25 [29]: Ch 1, sc in first st, ch 2, dc dec in next 2 sts, dc in each st across to last 2 sts, dc dec in last 2 sts, turn. *(42 dc)*

Rows 26–32 [30–36]: Ch 1, sc in first st, ch 2, [dc dec in next 2 sts] twice, dc in each st across to last 4 sts, [dc dec in next 2 sts] twice, turn. At end of last row, fasten off. *(14 sts at end of last row)*

Rnd 33 [37]: Working in sts and in ends of rows around outer edge, join off-white with sc in row 18 at right back corner, sc in each st, sc in each sc row, 3 sc in each tr row and 2 sc in each dc row around, **join** *(see Pattern Notes)* in beg sc, turn. *(164 [180] sc)*

Row 34 [38]: Now working in rows, ch 1, sc in each of first 140 [156] sts, leave last 24 sts unworked, turn. *(140 [156] sc)*

Row 35 [39]: Ch 1, sc in each st across, turn.

Row 36 [40]: Ch 1, sc in each of first 29 [33] sts, **sc dec** *(see Stitch Guide)* in next 2 sts, *sc in each of next 18 [20] sts, sc dec in next 2 sts, rep from * 3 times, sc in each of last 29 [33] sts, turn. *(135 [151] sc)*

Row 37 [41]: Hold elastic over sts of last row, leaving excess extended at each end; working over elastic *(see Fig. 2)*, ch 1, sc in each st across. Fasten off.

Fig. 2
Single Crochet Around Elastic Into Stitches

FINISHING
TIE
Join off-white in 1 end of row 37 [41], ch 43, sl st in 2nd ch from hook and in each ch across, join in same row. Fasten off.

Rep on opposite end of row 37 [41].

Place Cover on lid, pull ends of elastic, gathering to fit. Leaving ¾-inch elastic at each end, cut off excess elastic. Fold ends under, sew to back to secure.

RUG
SKILL LEVEL

INTERMEDIATE

FINISHED SIZE
22 x 42 inches, including Fringe

MATERIALS
- Medium (worsted) weight yarn:
  20 oz/1,000 yds/567g off-white
  6 oz/300 yds/170g buff
  4 oz/200 yds/113g each carrot,
    light coral, dark blue and country blue
- Size I/9/5.5mm crochet hook
  or size needed to obtain gauge

- Rustproof pins
- Yardstick
- Steam iron or garment steamer

GAUGE
With 2 strands of yarn held tog: 5 sts = 2 inches; 4 dc rows = 3 inches

PATTERN NOTES
Use rug backing on back of rugs that are placed on floors other than carpet.

Hold 2 strands of yarn together unless otherwise stated.

For easier handling of yarn when changing colors, using 2 strands of yarn held together, wind 2 small balls each of carrot and light coral to be used for diamond.

When changing colors, always change in last stitch made.

Single crochet and chain-1 at beginning of row or round counts as first half double crochet unless otherwise stated.

Chain-3 at beginning of row or round **does not** count as first double crochet unless otherwise stated.

INSTRUCTIONS
RUG
CENTER DIAMOND PANEL
Row 1 (RS): With 2 strands off-white held tog *(see Pattern Notes)*, ch 56, **sc in 2nd ch from hook, ch 1** *(see Pattern Notes)*, hdc in each ch across, turn. *(55 hdc)*

Rows 2 & 3: Ch 1, sc in first st, ch 1, hdc in each of next 25 sts **changing colors** *(see Stitch Guide and Pattern Notes)* to 2 strands carrot in last st, drop last color to WS of work, pick up as needed; when changing colors, always drop yarn on same side of work; hdc in each of next 3 sts changing to 2 strands off-white in last st, hdc in each of rem last 26 sts, turn.

Rows 4 & 5: Ch 1, sc in first st, ch 1, hdc in each of next 22 sts changing to carrot in last st, hdc in each of next 3 sts changing to light coral in last st, hdc in each of next 3 sts changing to carrot in last st, hdc in each of next 3 sts changing to off-white in last st, hdc in each of rem last 23 sts, turn.

Rows 6 & 7: Ch 1, sc in first st, ch 1, hdc in each of next 19 sts changing to carrot in last st, hdc in each of next 3 sts changing to light coral in last st, hdc in each of next 9 sts changing to carrot in last st, hdc in each of next 3 sts changing to off-white in last st, hdc in rem last 20 sts, turn.

Rows 8 & 9: Ch 1, sc in first st, ch 1, hdc in each of next 16 sts changing to carrot in last st, hdc in each of next 3 sts changing to light coral in last st, hdc in each of next 6 sts changing to blue in last st, hdc in each of next 3 sts changing to light coral in last st, hdc in next 6 sts changing to carrot in last st, hdc in each of next 3 sts changing to off-white in last st, hdc in each of rem last 17 sts, turn.

Rows 10 & 11: Rep rows 6 and 7.

Rows 12 & 13: Rep rows 4 and 5.

Rows 14 & 15: Rep rows 2 and 3.

Row 16: Ch 1, sc in first st, ch 1, hdc in each of rem last sts across, turn.

Row 17: Ch 1, sc in first st, ch 2, dc in each st across, **do not turn**. Fasten off.

FIRST SIDE

Row 18: Join carrot with **fpsc** (see Stitch Guide) around first dc on last row, ch 2, **bpdc** (see Stitch Guide) around each of rem last sts across, **do not turn**. Fasten off.

Row 19: With country blue, rep row 18.

Row 20: With dark blue, rep row 18.

Row 21: With light coral, rep row 18.

Row 22: Join buff with fpsc around first dc on last row, ch 2, bpdc around each of last rem sts of row, turn. **Do not fasten off**.

Row 23: Ch 1, sc in each st across, turn. Fasten off.

Row 24: Sk first st, join carrot with sc in next st, ch 2, tr in next st, [ch 1, sk next st, tr in each of next 2 sts] 17 times, sk last st, **do not turn**. Fasten off.

Row 25: Join buff with sc in first sk st on row before last, ch 3, [sc in each of next 2 sts, working in front of ch-1, tr in next sk st on row before last] 18 times, **do not turn**. Fasten off.

Row 26: Join buff with sc in first st, ch 2, dc in each of rem last sts across, **do not turn**. Fasten off.

Row 27: With light coral, rep row 18.

Row 28: With dark blue, rep row 18.

Row 29: With country blue, rep row 18.

Row 30: With carrot, rep row 18.

Row 31: Join off-white with fpsc around first dc on last row, ch 2, bpdc around each of rem last sts of row, turn. **Do not fasten off**.

Rows 32–37: Ch 1, sc in first st, ch 2, dc in each of rem last sts across, turn. At end of last row, fasten off.

2ND SIDE

Row 38: Working in starting ch on opposite side of row 1, with RS facing, join off-white with sc in first ch, ch 2, dc in each of rem last chs across, **do not turn**. Fasten off.

Rows 39–58: Rep rows 18–37 of First Side.

FINISHING

To block Rug, pin corners and sides of Rug on a padded surface, using yardstick as a guide for straightening edges.

Steam with iron or garment steamer, being careful iron does not touch yarn.

Allow to dry completely before removing pins.

To keep edges smooth and even, with tapestry needle and off-white, whipstitch across ends of post stitch rows on each side of Rug.

FRINGE

Cut 6 strands off-white, each strand 11 inches long. With all 6 strands held tog, fold in half, insert hook in st, pull fold through st, pull ends through fold, tighten.

Attach Fringe in every other st across each end of Rug.

TISSUE ROLL COVER
SKILL LEVEL

INTERMEDIATE

FINISHED SIZE

Fits 4½-inch-diameter roll of bath tissue

MATERIALS

- Medium (worsted) weight yarn: 1 oz/50 yds/28g each off-white, buff, carrot, dark blue and country blue
- Size H/8/5mm crochet hook or size needed to obtain gauge

4 MEDIUM

GAUGE

10 dc = 3 inches; 5 dc rows = 3 inches

PATTERN NOTES

Single crochet and chain-2 at beginning of row or round counts as first double crochet unless otherwise stated.

Chain-3 at beginning of row or round **does not** count as first double crochet unless otherwise stated.

Join with slip stitch as indicated unless otherwise stated.

INSTRUCTIONS
COVER
TOP

Rnd 1: With off-white, ch 4, 11 dc in 4th ch from hook (*first 3 chs count as first dc*), **join** (*see Pattern Notes*) in 3rd ch of beg ch-4. (*12 dc*)

Rnd 2: Ch 1, **sc in first st, ch 2** (*see Pattern Notes*), 2 dc in each st around, dc in same st as beg sc, join 2nd ch of beg ch-2. (*24 dc*)

Rnd 3: Ch 1, sc in first st, ch 2, dc in next st, [2 dc in next st, dc in next st] around, dc in same st as beg sc, join in 2nd ch of beg ch-2. (*36 dc*)

Rnd 4: Ch 1, sc in first st, ch 2, dc in each of next 2 sts, [2 dc in next st, dc in each of next 2 sts] around, dc in same st as beg sc, join in 2nd ch of beg ch-2. Fasten off. (*48 dc*)

SIDE

Rnd 1: With buff, ch 48, working in **back bar of ch** *(see Fig. 1)*, sl st in first ch to form ring, ch 1, sc in first ch, ch 2, dc in each ch around, join in 2nd ch of beg ch-2. *(48 dc)*

Fig. 1
Back Bar of Chain

Rnd 2: Ch 1, sc in each st around join in beg sc. Fasten off.

Rnd 3: Join carrot with sc in first st on last rnd, ch 3, tr in next st, ch 1, sk next st, [tr in each of next 2 sts, ch 1, sk next st] around, join in 3rd ch of beg ch-3.

Rnd 4: Join buff with sc in first st on last rnd, sc in next st, working in front of ch-1, tr in sk st on rnd before last, [sc in each of next 2 sts, working in front of ch-1, tr in sk st on rnd before last] around, join in beg sc. **Do not fasten off.**

Rnd 5: Ch 1, sc in first st, ch 2, dc in each st around, join in 2nd ch of beg ch-2. Fasten off.

Rnd 6: Join dark blue with **fpsc** *(see Stitch Guide)* around first dc on last rnd, ch 2, **bpdc** *(see Stitch Guide)* around each of rem last sts join in 2nd ch of beg ch-2. Fasten off.

Rnd 7: With country blue, rep rnd 6.

Rnd 8: With carrot, rep rnd 6.

Rnd 9: Working in starting ch on opposite side of rnd 1, join with fpsc around post of first dc, ch 2, bpdc around each of rem last sts of rnd, join in 2nd ch of beg ch-2. Fasten off.

Rnd 10: With country blue, rep rnd 6.

Rnd 11: With carrot, rep rnd 6.

FINISHING

With Side piece facing, hold Side and Top WS tog, matching sts of rnd 4 on Top and rnd 8 on Side, working through both thicknesses, join

carrot with sl st in any st, sl st in each st around, join in beg sc. Fasten off.

BOUTIQUE TISSUE COVER
SKILL LEVEL

◼◼◼◻
INTERMEDIATE

FINISHED SIZE

Fits 4½ x 5¼-inch boutique tissue box

MATERIALS

- Medium (worsted) weight yarn: 1 oz/50 yds/28g each off-white, buff, carrot, light coral, dark blue and country blue
- Size H/8/5mm crochet hook or size needed to obtain gauge

4 MEDIUM

GAUGE

10 dc = 3 inches; 5 dc rows = 3 inches

PATTERN NOTES

Single crochet and chain-2 at beginning of row or round counts as first double crochet unless otherwise stated.

Chain-3 at beginning of row or round **does not** count as first double crochet unless otherwise stated.

Join with slip stitch as indicated unless otherwise stated.

INSTRUCTIONS
COVER
TOP

Rnd 1: With off-white, ch 28, working in **back bar of ch** *(see Fig. 1)*, sl st in first ch to form ring, ch 1, **sc in same ch, ch 2** *(see Pattern Notes)*, 4 dc in same ch as first dc, dc in each of next 6 chs, [5 dc in next ch, dc in each of next 6 chs] around, **join** *(see Pattern Notes)* in 2nd ch of beg ch-2. *(44 dc)*

Fig. 1
Back Bar of Chain

Rnd 2: Ch 1, sc in first st, ch 2, 2 dc in next st, 3 tr in next st, 2 dc in next st, [dc in each of next 8 sts, 2 dc in next st, 3 tr in next st, 2 dc in next st] 3 times, dc in each of last 7 sts, join in 2nd ch of beg ch-2. *(60 dc)*

SIDES

Rnd 1: With buff, ch 60, working in back bar of ch, sl st in first ch to form ring, ch 1, sc in first ch, ch 2, dc in each ch around, join in 2nd ch of beg ch-2. *(60 dc)*

Rnd 2: Ch 1, sc in each st around, join in beg sc. Fasten off.

Rnd 3: Join carrot with sc in first st on last rnd, ch 3, tr in next st, ch 1, sk next st, [tr in each of next 2 sts, ch 1, sk next st] around, join in 3rd ch of beg ch-3. Fasten off.

Rnd 4: Join buff with sc in first st on last rnd, sc in next st, working in front of ch-1, tr in next sk st on rnd before last, [sc in each of next 2 sts, working in front of ch-1, tr in next sk st on rnd before last] around, join in beg sc. **Do not fasten off.**

Rnd 5: Ch 1, sc in first st, ch 2, dc in each of rem last sts around, join in 2nd ch of beg ch-2. Fasten off.

Rnd 6: Join light coral with **fpsc** *(see Stitch Guide)* around first dc on last rnd, ch 2, **bpdc** *(see Stitch Guide)* around each of rem last sts, join in 2nd ch of beg ch-2. Fasten off.

Rnd 7: With dark blue, rep rnd 6.

Rnd 8: With country blue, rep rnd 6.

Rnd 9: With carrot, rep rnd 6.

Rnd 10: Working in starting ch on opposite side of rnd 1, join light coral with fpsc around first dc, ch 2, bpdc around each of rem last sts, join in 2nd ch of beg ch-2.

Rnd 11: With dark blue, rep rnd 6.

Rnd 12: With country blue, rep rnd 6.

Rnd 13: With carrot, rep rnd 6.

FINISHING

With Side piece facing, hold Side and Top WS tog, matching sts of rnd 2 on Top and rnd 9 on Side, working through both thicknesses, join carrot with sl st in any st, sl st in each st around, join in beg sl st. Fasten off. ∎

Stitch Guide

For more complete information, visit **FreePatterns.com**

ABBREVIATIONS

beg	begin/begins/beginning
bpdc	back post double crochet
bpsc	back post single crochet
bptr	back post treble crochet
CC	contrasting color
ch(s)	chain(s)
ch-	refers to chain or space previously made (e.g., ch-1 space)
ch sp(s)	chain space(s)
cl(s)	cluster(s)
cm	centimeter(s)
dc	double crochet (singular/plural)
dc dec	double crochet 2 or more stitches together, as indicated
dec	decrease/decreases/decreasing
dtr	double treble crochet
ext	extended
fpdc	front post double crochet
fpsc	front post single crochet
fptr	front post treble crochet
g	gram(s)
hdc	half double crochet
hdc dec	half double crochet 2 or more stitches together, as indicated
inc	increase/increases/increasing
lp(s)	loop(s)
MC	main color
mm	millimeter(s)
oz	ounce(s)
pc	popcorn(s)
rem	remain/remains/remaining
rep(s)	repeat(s)
rnd(s)	round(s)
RS	right side
sc	single crochet (singular/plural)
sc dec	single crochet 2 or more stitches together, as indicated
sk	skip/skipped/skipping
sl st(s)	slip stitch(es)
sp(s)	space/spaces/spaced
st(s)	stitch(es)
tog	together
tr	treble crochet
trtr	triple treble
WS	wrong side
yd(s)	yard(s)
yo	yarn over

Chain—ch: Yo, pull through lp on hook.

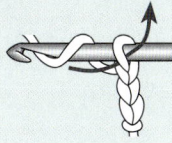

Slip stitch—sl st: Insert hook in st, pull through both lps on hook.

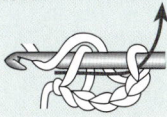

Single crochet—sc: Insert hook in st, yo, pull through st, yo, pull through both lps on hook.

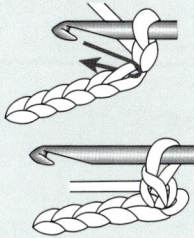

Front post stitch—fp: Back post stitch—bp: When working post st, insert hook from right to left around post st on previous row.

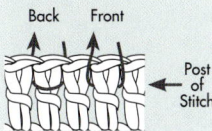

Back Front

Post of Stitch

Front loop—front lp Back loop—back lp

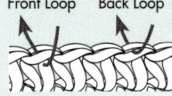

Front Loop   Back Loop

Half double crochet—hdc: Yo, insert hook in st, yo, pull through st, yo, pull through all 3 lps on hook.

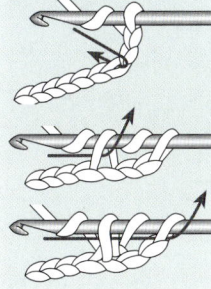

Double crochet—dc: Yo, insert hook in st, yo, pull through st, [yo, pull through 2 lps] twice.

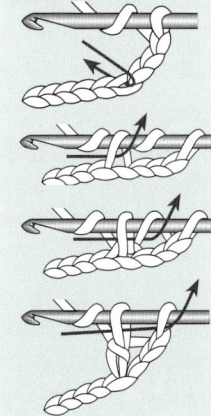

Change colors: Drop first color; with 2nd color, pull through last 2 lps of st.

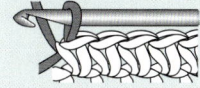

Treble crochet—tr: Yo twice, insert hook in st, yo, pull through st, [yo, pull through 2 lps] 3 times.

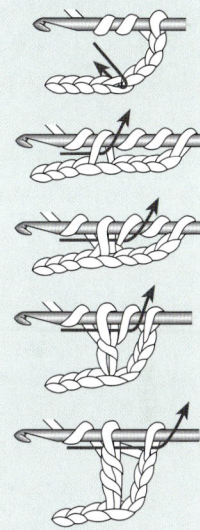

Double treble crochet—dtr: Yo 3 times, insert hook in st, yo, pull through st, [yo, pull through 2 lps] 4 times.

Single crochet decrease (sc dec): (Insert hook, yo, draw lp through) in each of the sts indicated, yo, draw through all lps on hook.

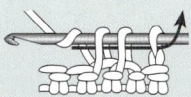

Example of 2-sc dec

Half double crochet decrease (hdc dec): (Yo, insert hook, yo, draw lp through) in each of the sts indicated, yo, draw through all lps on hook.

Example of 2-hdc dec

Double crochet decrease (dc dec): (Yo, insert hook, yo, draw loop through, draw through 2 lps on hook) in each of the sts indicated, yo, draw through all lps on hook.

Example of 2-dc dec

Treble crochet decrease (tr dec): Holding back last lp of each st, tr in each of the sts indicated, yo, pull through all lps on hook.

Example of 2-tr dec

US		UK	
sl st (slip stitch)	=	sc (single crochet)	
sc (single crochet)	=	dc (double crochet)	
hdc (half double crochet)	=	htr (half treble crochet)	
dc (double crochet)	=	tr (treble crochet)	
tr (treble crochet)	=	dtr (double treble crochet)	
dtr (double treble crochet)	=	ttr (triple treble crochet)	
skip	=	miss	

Metric
Conversion
Charts

METRIC CONVERSIONS

yards	x	.9144	=	metres (m)
yards	x	91.44	=	centimetres (cm)
inches	x	2.54	=	centimetres (cm)
inches	x	25.40	=	millimetres (mm)
inches	x	.0254	=	metres (m)

centimetres	x	.3937	=	inches
metres	x	1.0936	=	yards

INCHES INTO MILLIMETRES & CENTIMETRES (Rounded off slightly)

inches	mm	cm	inches	cm	inches	cm	inches	cm
1/8	3	0.3	5	12.5	21	53.5	38	96.5
1/4	6	0.6	5 1/2	14	22	56	39	99
3/8	10	1	6	15	23	58.5	40	101.5
1/2	13	1.3	7	18	24	61	41	104
5/8	15	1.5	8	20.5	25	63.5	42	106.5
3/4	20	2	9	23	26	66	43	109
7/8	22	2.2	10	25.5	27	68.5	44	112
1	25	2.5	11	28	28	71	45	114.5
1 1/4	32	3.2	12	30.5	29	73.5	46	117
1 1/2	38	3.8	13	33	30	76	47	119.5
1 3/4	45	4.5	14	35.5	31	79	48	122
2	50	5	15	38	32	81.5	49	124.5
2 1/2	65	6.5	16	40.5	33	84	50	127
3	75	7.5	17	43	34	86.5		
3 1/2	90	9	18	46	35	89		
4	100	10	19	48.5	36	91.5		
4 1/2	115	11.5	20	51	37	94		

KNITTING NEEDLES CONVERSION CHART

Canada/U.S.	0	1	2	3	4	5	6	7	8	9	10	10½	11	13	15
Metric (mm)	2	2¼	2¾	3¼	3½	3¾	4	4½	5	5½	6	6½	8	9	10

CROCHET HOOKS CONVERSION CHART

Canada/U.S.	1/B	2/C	3/D	4/E	5/F	6/G	8/H	9/I	10/J	10½/K	N
Metric (mm)	2.25	2.75	3.25	3.5	3.75	4.25	5	5.5	6	6.5	9.0

Annie's Attic®

TOLL-FREE ORDER LINE or to request a free catalog (800) LV-ANNIE (800) 582-6643
Customer Service (800) AT-ANNIE (800) 282-6643, **Fax** (800) 882-6643
Visit AnniesAttic.com
We have made every effort to ensure the accuracy and completeness of these instructions.
We cannot, however, be responsible for human error, typographical mistakes or variations in individual work.

ISBN: 978-1-59635-246-9

1 2 3 4 5 6 7 8 9